SUMMER HOUSES

SUMMER HOUSES

A Change in Perspective

Izabela Anna Moren

We all experience summer, and it often brings a sense of expectation and anticipation. For some, there are traditions to be respected and repeated each year: booking a familiar house, returning to a beloved island, or reconnecting with friends and family in the warm embrace of consistency and routine. For others, the summer is a time to break free and go somewhere completely new—to dazzle the brain and body with novel impressions that will continue to nourish the spirit long after the season ends.

But what makes a great summer home, and what sets it apart from other houses? The examples in this book, all so different from one another, make it clear that a perfect summer dwelling isn't about size—it doesn't have to be bigger than our usual home. It is not about location, either; it could be close by or as far away as possible. Nor is it about budget: luxury is not a key element of the perennial experience called summer, often best appreciated with only the essentials.

Some of us experience warm weather or the seaside as part of daily life, not a rare vacation feature. This is the case for me, as I have lived in Palermo, Sicily, for the past seven years, and yet I wouldn't define my house here as a summer home. In fact, for many people (not for me), summer means fresh mountain air, forest views, and plunges into ice-cold lakes. Often, when we look for a summer house, what we are searching for is not—or at least, not only—a change in location. What the summer dwelling must offer is a change in perspective.

The architects and studios featured here have created environments that meet both those needs. Every dwelling, no matter its specific characteristics, provides at its core a space for observation. The cultures we inhabit daily ask us to follow routines, and the spaces we normally occupy are structured accordingly; we condition them, and they condition us. The places we turn to in order to disrupt these routines are very different. They are more experimental, encourage a deeper connection with nature, and allow us to dream of another way of living. They are not symbols of luxury but necessary resets of who we are—architectural dreamscapes where we can reflect in solitude or spend precious time with others, recharge, and test out different personas. When it is time to return home, we do so nurtured by the air, sun, and emptiness embedded in the very fabric of the dwellings we have chosen, or sometimes that others have chosen for us. This may be another defining feature of the vacation house: It is usually inhabited in company. Even the smallest dwelling on the following pages can welcome at least two inhabitants.

My best summers have been spent on the small island of Alicudi. A few hours by boat from Palermo, Italy, it has a population of only thirty, though that number naturally rises during the warmer months. I have been able to enjoy this specific place because the parents of a friend, an architect–interior designer couple, renovated a crumbling ruin far up on a hill, a spot that only a few lucky and enlightened foreigners have chosen for their summer houses. There is one shop selling groceries, another that mainly focuses on tobacco, a bar offering icy granita and evening drinks, and a few home restaurants that welcome travelers, benefiting from the seasonal economy and the encounters with strangers that it brings. A few local women sell salted capers by the kilo, and fishermen can be intercepted in the mornings but need to be convinced to sell. To reach all these amenities, visitors must hike across various steep sets of crumbling steps and dry-stone walls. Goats greet while sweat drips.

The scenery—easily reimagined with each of these fifty homes in locations as diverse as the mountain environment of Argentina, Harbour Island in the Bahamas, coastal villages in Chile, the Greek Cyclades archipelago, deserted beaches near the urban bustle of Lagos, or the famous Cap Ferrat in France—takes shape through materials as varied and elemental as the homes and landscapes themselves: rock, glass, wood, concrete. No rules or generalizations can be made about the summer home; too personal and diverse is the range of perfect solutions that can be applied.

Turning these pages, one drifts into admiring the different architectural and conceptual approaches ranging from pools, outdoor spaces,and gardens to structural engineering such as stilts and off-the-grid appliances. Color palettes include everything from neon tiles to earth-toned plaster. Attention to detail, distinctive qualities, and the possibility afforded by experimentation—without needing to please anybody but the client—render the houses collected here a valuable source of inspiration, and possibly a manual of interventions and strategies to adopt, copy, and try out elsewhere.

In nearly every case, sustainability emerges as a central priority, both desired by clients and met with consideration by the architects. Light is carefully measured and windows are placed to avoid excessive heat, with openings calculated to offer the right amount of breeze and ventilation; foundations are planned on elevations or stilts to avoid disturbing the land. Extensive efforts have been made to render the relationship between humans and other inhabitants as harmonious as possible.

Flipping through the pages naturally invites the reader to imagine spending time in many of the projects featured. Whether set in the rainforest, perched on a rocky island, high on a mountainside, or deep in a Nordic forest, each one prompts us to reflect on how it might feel to be there—making the experience of this book something like a small summer vacation in itself.

Sinfonia Verde, 2022
Peninsula de Osa, Puntarenas Province, Costa Rica

Studio Saxe

On the site where a large tree once fell, clearing a spot of land in the jungle, a new home has arisen. Due to its challenging location—difficult to reach, deep in the rainforest, with high precipitation and threatening wildlife—all construction materials had to be transported down a nearby river and carried to the site. As the build required extensive knowledge of everything from seasonal weather to transportation networks, a local construction firm was brought in to realize the building. The home extends over a single level with a central opening to a courtyard, offering respite from the jungle wildlife. A perimeter walkway and shaded outdoor spaces connect its two bedrooms, open-plan living room and kitchen, and research library. A hyperbolic roof structure shelters the home from the region's intense rains, channeling water down the roof in cascades and into natural streams. As the owners are conscious of the environment—they propagate native plant species and engage in initiatives to restore nearby coral reefs—sustainability was a key consideration in the design process. Raising the dwelling on stilts permitted the preservation of groundwater flows and root systems while minimizing the disturbance to animals inhabiting the land. Passive ventilation responds to the extreme heat and humidity of the area, while the white roof deflects sunlight away. The residents generate power from photovoltaic systems, and a hydroturbine installed at a nearby stream supplies the home with drinking water. Responsibly sourced teak and cork blend with the surrounding nature and complete the sustainable design mission.

Concrete House by the Ocean, 2023
Nasugbu, Batangas, Philippines

MB Architecture Studio

Perched on a cliffside overlooking the South China Sea, Micaela Benedicto's Concrete House by the Ocean lives up to its name. The brutalist construction by MB Architecture Studio, situated in Nasugbu—within a region known for aquaculture, tourism, and the cultivation of sugarcane, rice, fruit, vegetables and, coconut—is an open-air pavilion. Boundaries between interior and exterior spaces are blurred to a maximum through its strategic placement on the highest point of the plot, which makes it at times seem as if one were on the sea. The concrete was cast in situ using recycled wooden planks, giving the dwelling a rough yet uniform appearance. A main volume in the middle serves as a long, open-plan living area that can be fully opened to the elements, the terrace, and the poolside via retractable glazing on both sides. Above, the roof doubles as a viewing deck, offering breathtaking vistas of ocean and sky. Flanking the central living space are two discreet volumes housing the bedrooms, while the lower ground floor accommodates a caretaker's quarters and utility area. The use of concrete ledges throughout protects from the region's heat and rain. While the absence of exterior ceilings or wall finishes may seem like a purely aesthetic choice, it is also a strategy that ensures longevity and low maintenance, as such elements could deteriorate in the humid seaside climate. The thoughtful design and material choices continue on the inside with smooth concrete flooring, exposed wall details, modern furniture, and understated fixtures, ensuring that the panorama remains the protagonist.

Casa GR, 2022
Lago Riñihue, Región de los Ríos, Chile

Tomás de Iruarrizaga

On the shores of Riñihue Lake, a glacial lake in southern Chile, Casa GR, designed by architect Tomás de Iruarrizaga, provides impeccable conditions for year-round living. The 5,400-ft^2 (500-m^2) home is a family retreat with enough space for relaxation, socializing, and work. Its form resembles a ranch house, but its construction is unusual: Two reinforced concrete rectangles stand separately on the ground floor, and a cross-laminated timber structure bridges them to create the upper floor. Upstairs, large windows on all sides allow for breathtaking views of the lake and the Mocho-Choshuenco volcano, a glacier-covered compound volcano that has erupted in the past but is now considered dormant. Wood dominates the interiors. The cross-laminated structure has been left exposed and is clad with more wood to create a light, natural atmosphere. Wooden furnishings and a large wood-burning fireplace complete the holiday feeling in the generous open-plan living room, adjacent to the kitchen, dining room, and additional bedrooms on the same floor. The layout is organized to offer communal and private spaces, ensuring comfort and intimacy while panoramas of snowcapped mountains and light reflecting on the lake remain always in sight. Below, the concrete volume is separated by an outdoor space that extends onto the patio, inviting gatherings and contemplation. It houses the more secluded master bedrooms. De Iruarrizaga specializes in homes in remote, difficult, or otherwise extreme places, so it comes as no surprise that this dwelling is perfectly situated without overimposing on its natural context.

Caochan na Creige, 2023
Isle of Harris, Scotland, UK

Izat Arundell

Caochan na Creige, meaning "little quiet one by the rock" in Gaelic, is a poetic and resilient home situated on the Isle of Harris in Scotland's Outer Hebrides, one of the most fascinating destinations in Britain. It marks the debut project of emerging practice Izat Arundell, prioritizing natural construction materials and a profound connection to the untouched landscape. The house is designed around the substantial Lewisian Gneiss stone, a rock formation of Archaean and Paleoproterozoic origins, ranging from 1.7 to 3.0 billion years old. It became a defining feature of the site, informing the home's distinctive shape, in which a soft 135-degree angle is repeated throughout the layout. Rather than working against the rock, the design applies a site-specific approach to include it. The house was built by Jack Arundell, Eilidh Izat, her brother Alasdair Izat, and stonemason Dan Macaulay and the construction process was a complex collaboration that spanned eighteen months, during which the team overcame several hurdles, including nine named storms. Despite a modest budget, the team picked local materials to strengthen the building's connection with the landscape. Its timber-frame structure is clad in traditional full-thickness Lewisian Gneiss sourced from a nearby quarry, while the walls feature a concrete "ring beam" cast in situ and washed back to expose the same Lewisian Gneiss aggregate. On the inside, the 915-ft^2 (85-m^2) home is organized in an open-plan layout prioritizing spaciousness and vistas. The living room serves as the focal point of the home, boasting an cast-iron fireplace, rose-colored modern tiles, and an extensive panorama of the rocks and sea. Scottish cedar cladding lends the interiors a warm and intimate character, in line with the sanctuary-like nature of the entire project.

Lover's House, 2020
Santa María del Camí, Mallorca, Spain

Isla Architects

The skeleton of an unfinished house was offered to the architects to produce an unconventional project for the client to sell. On a site in the island's less inhabited middle area, mostly dedicated to agriculture, Isla Architects reimagined a reuse strategy for the existing basement and building foundations. The architects revised everything, from wall openings to a complete reworking of the palette and materials. Approached through the surrounding pine forest, the rough, rust-colored house emerges as a closed entity; a large floor-to-ceiling door pivots open to reveal an unexpectedly bright interior. Aspects of the design, including the color and the transition from closed to open, are inspired by the island's Arab heritage. Inside, a nearly monochromatic palette of red-tinted concrete, white plaster, copper, and natural wood continues. It makes use of more washed-out, subtle hues, such as the hydraulic floor tiles—expertly crafted by Huguet Mallorca especially for the project—that run throughout. Everything is custom-made, including benches, sinks, shelves, the fireplace, and even the chimney; all feature the muted red tones and thoughtfully chosen shapes and dimensions that define the building. Various patios and large openings frame views of the Serra de Tramuntana and vineyards, introducing natural light and connecting the dwelling to exterior spaces while dividing the house into distinct zones: a guest suite, main living areas, a kitchen. A long pool completes the holiday feeling on the outside, slightly secluded and running parallel to the house and terrace, it provides a pleasant view of the rust- and rose-colored palette.

Summer House, 2023
Lake Balaton, Tihany, Hungary

RAPA

Occupying the undulating landscape of Hungary's Balaton Uplands, the RAPA Summer House stands as a quiet ode to vernacular heritage and material honesty. Drawing from the local rural architecture, the house is characterized by its hand-laid stone base and a steeply pitched, thatched roof—evoking traditional peasant cottages yet distilled through a contemporary lens. The structure comprises two intersecting volumes with contrasting locally sourced materials. A long, stone-built base houses bedrooms and auxiliary spaces. A soaring gabled form, defined by its roof thatched with reeds harvested from the lake, shelters the double-height living area, which is flooded by light through its glazed southeast facade. This particular spatial organization, with sauna, bathing area, and terrace nestled on the middle storey, creates a dynamic interplay between compression and release, intimacy and openness. Large, strategically placed apertures frame the surrounding vineyards and volcanic hills, firmly grounding the family within its context. One of the elements that sets the project apart is its attention to craftsmanship. Locally sourced stone was dry-laid by regional masons, while the thatching—a disappearing art—was executed by one of Hungary's few remaining master thatchers. Internally, minimal interventions and a subdued palette allow natural light and diverse textures to dominate. Custom-built wooden furniture complements the raw finishes, creating a warm, timeless environment. This summer house is not merely a retreat but a nuanced architectural statement. By reclaiming and refining indigenous building techniques, RAPA Architects offers a compelling vision of sustainable, place-based design in the twenty-first century.

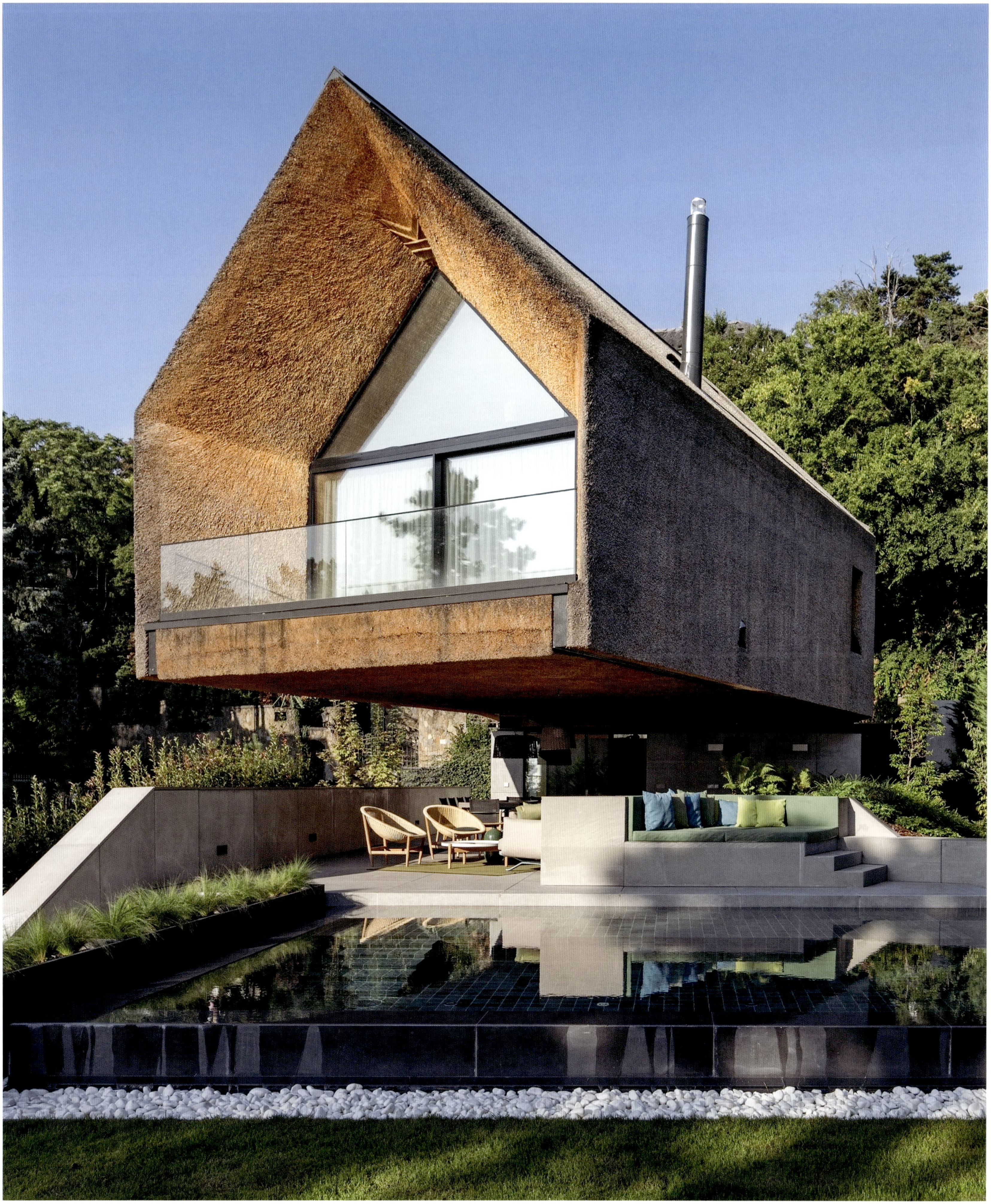

Canopy House, 2023
Prainha Branca, Guarujá, São Paulo, Brazil

Studio MK27

On a steeply sloping hillside in Guarujá, within Brazil's Atlantic Forest, Canopy House by Studio MK27 exemplifies a harmonious fusion of architecture and nature. After thorough consideration of access points, views, and feasibility, the architects raised the 8,500-ft^2 (785-m^2) residence on stilts, minimizing disruption to the site's topography. Although only a two-hour drive from the city of São Paulo, this is a tropical rainforest setting with thick, lush foliage. The design takes this into consideration with an external spiral staircase leading from the ground-floor bedrooms to the main living areas, necessarily immersing inhabitants in the surrounding jungle environment. The residence is laid out to meet the needs of three generations. Service areas and a sauna are situated in the basement, bedrooms on the ground floor, and a bright, open-plan living area on the first floor, opening onto an outdoor deck and pool. As the dwelling forms an overhanging canopy supported by concrete columns, the lower volume has the smallest footprint. Gardens and outdoor platforms surround the building, connecting the columns, concrete, and other architectural features to the jungle in Brazilian Modernist style. The interiors showcase a curated selection of Brazilian contemporary design, traditional craftsmanship, and artworks from the owners' collection. The material palette is minimal, with concrete, pine timber, and basalt stone. There is a subtle distinction in style between outdoors and indoors, with the constant presence of nature outside rendering the inside spaces more homey. A custom-made *cobogó* lattice adds natural ventilation and casts ever-changing shadows on walls and floors.

Summer House in Mesaria, 2024
Mesaria, Santorini, Greece

Kapsimalis Architects

Kapsimalis Architects' Summer House in Mesaria is a masterful blend of heritage and modernity. Situated on the outskirts of the traditional village of Mesaria, this project transforms a historic subterranean wine cellar, known as a *canava*, into a contemporary summer home. The original vaulted spaces, winepress, and cisterns have been preserved as part of the new home typology, maintaining the building's historical character. All flows seamlessly in the new layout. In the main vaulted area, now serving as an open-plan living room and bedroom, built-in furniture and benches unite walls, furniture, and flooring with a pleasantly simple and Mediterranean flair. Restored wine cellar artifacts are thoughtfully incorporated into the adjacent space, which retains its kitchen function, while new materials such as smooth terrazzo floors, white cement plaster, and minimalist furniture introduce a contemporary aesthetic. A sensitive restoration approach, balancing tradition with modern sensibility, has created a refined, simple, and elegant retreat. The design also emphasizes a gentle color palette with earth and gray tones on the inside that stand out against the classic whitewashed facades of Santorini on the outside. A new lightweight pergola in the enclosed yard provides an exterior dining area, directly extending the inner space to the outdoors. An existing staircase now leads to a tiered terrace with a small pool, ideal for observing the surroundings or retreating in contemplative silence. With natural materials and minimal fixtures, the design bridges history and modern living.

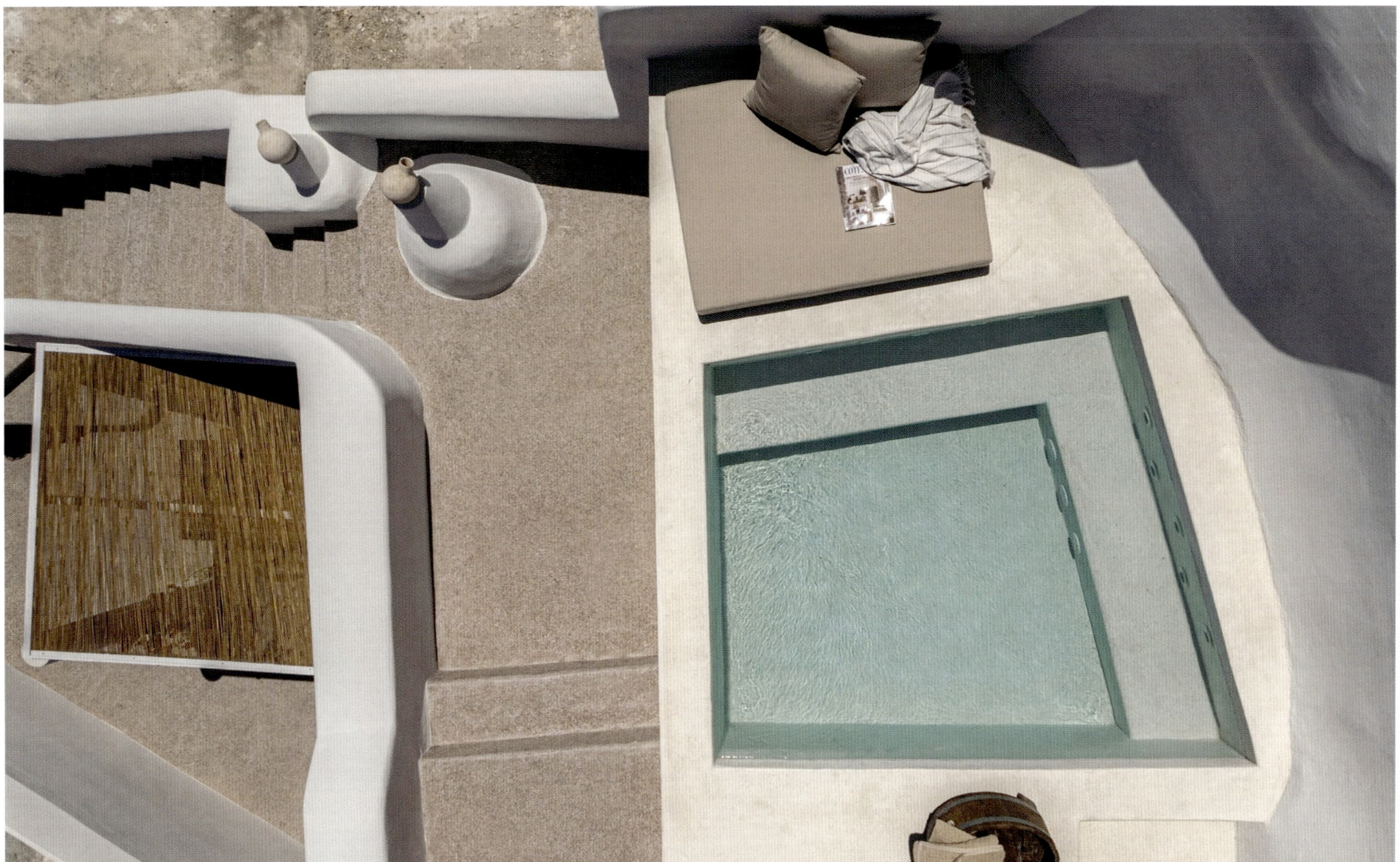

Copper Bottom, 2024
Oxford, England, UK

Adrian James Architects

Located on the edge of Oxford, England, overlooking the city's green belt, Copper Bottom is an unexpected and visionary summer house by Adrian James Architects. As critic Rowan Moore points out in his *Guardian* review of the property, most dwellings designed with sustainability in mind are very visibly so, with a recurring aesthetic and choice of materials. In this case, understatement has been practiced while delivering shapes and colors completely out of the ordinary. The self-build, a home for the architect and his family, stands within a wildflower meadow. The starting point for its design was a compact form, a large roof oriented south, and an envelope that shelters large windows from the sun and prevents overheating. The building's playful cuboid form is an interpretation of these basic needs. A green-patinated copper shell—made with copper recycled from scrap and attached to plywood—clads the entire home and protects it from the sun, putting a twofold focus on eco-design. The origami-esque shape together with the greenish color make the structure resemble an animal or a postmodern machine for living, introducing an element of playfulness and joy to the landscape. An angled roof plane that cantilevers and creased bulges on the east and west facades are responsible for the funky shape. The building's sustainability is further bolstered by thirty-seven photovoltaic panels on the roof, an air-source heat pump, triple-glazed windows, and generous insulation. These elements enable the house to generate more energy than it consumes, achieving a carbon payback period of just ten to fifteen years.

Horsö, 2022
Kalmar, Sweden

Bross + Nick Flygt

On Sweden's southeast coast, sitting between the historic city of Kalmarsund and a protected nature reserve overlooking the Baltic Sea, the Horsö summer house by Stockholm-based architects Bross and Nick Flygt is an understated retreat in harmony with its surroundings. Designed to accommodate a growing family, the 2,315-ft^2 (215-m^2) residence has a refined approach to Scandinavian minimalism that sits well in nature. The architectural composition features natural materials, including untreated timber, stone, and wood, chosen to let the structure age gracefully and patinate over time. This material palette, together with the flat roof and the horizontal development, reflects the architects' wish to disturb the surrounding landscape as little as possible. Structurally, a wooden framework sits atop a concrete foundation that has been elevated to anticipate potential rises in water levels.

Internally, smooth concrete floors and warm wooden surfaces coexist in elegant harmony. Large glass openings are set back into the facade, connecting the interior to a sheltered outdoor area and offering a gentle dialogue with the surrounding environment. Many details repeat consistently across roofs, columns, and the base, showcasing the meticulous attention of the architects, who work across architecture, interiors, and product design. The Horsö summer house's playful Japanese-inspired aesthetic is expressed through bespoke and freestanding furniture pieces that reflect Bross and Nick Flygt's commitment to craftsmanship and material experimentation. Red chairs and textile details mix with warm-hued wood, funky metal legs, and cladding, concentrating the design attention mainly on the interior of the project while letting the exterior engage with the natural environment.

Black Butte Residence, 2024
Sisters, Oregon, USA

LEVER Architecture

Built as a family retreat for an American entrepreneur who fell in love with Oregon's wilderness thirty years ago, the Black Butte Residence by LEVER Architecture stands on a forested site in the high desert landscape of central Oregon. The owners' deep connection to the site is reflected in their commitment to sustainability. The project translates the idea of a tent sitting lightly on a campsite into an architectural volume that preserves the family's favorite stargazing spot. The home's design is inspired by the surrounding Cascade Range, with each of the three main functions oriented to frame the view of a specific peak through the structure's split form. The bedroom to the north overlooks Black Butte, the south-oriented office gazes at the Three Fingered Jack, and the space above the two—an architectural meeting point that serves as a gathering space for the family—frames the famous Mount Jefferson, an inactive volcano. The lofty, glazed volumes allow for magnificent views, maximize light, and enhance comfort. Large, high-performance European triple-glazed windows capture natural light and ensure unobstructed views while reducing energy waste. An elegant and warmly spacious design prevails, featuring natural materials such as glue-laminated columns, Douglas fir ceilings, white oak floors, and custom millwork. Outside, dark-stained cedar siding and a black metal standing seam roof blend with the forested surroundings, lending the dwelling the character of a lodge despite its generous size. Highly insulated walls, roof, and floors contribute to the home's energy efficiency, and electric vehicle chargers help the residents reduce their fossil fuel use. A photovoltaic array offsets around 80 percent of the home's annual energy consumption.

HOMA, 2022
Vagia, Serifos, Greece

Mold Architects

Mass tourism has not yet arrived on Serifos, an island in the western Cyclades. On a site previously used for mining activities, a small boutique hotel is attempting to reimagine the island's industrial heritage. The resulting complex comprises three independent lodgings whose design ethos is rooted in the island's scarred landscape. Traces of past mining activities inform the architectural narrative, with the guiding idea being to revive a housing scenario belowground. Linear staircases are the only mode of access, descending from the roof toward the lodgings and into the landscape. Upon arrival, nothing gives away the existence of the light-filled and spacious apartments, with private pools, kitchens, and dining areas, which are to be found underneath the concrete terraces. The broad, flat surfaces created by the insertion of smooth concrete contrast with the rugged landscape and create pleasant experiences with patios, stairs, and pools that emerge from the subtraction of orthogonal volumes, allowing natural light and ventilation to permeate the spaces. Non-load-bearing brick walls have been coated in earthen pigmented plaster, giving them a warm, earthy hue that blends seamlessly with the surroundings. Beds, kitchens, and other furniture have been crafted from white polished concrete and pine wood, integrating everything into the architecture so that the dwellings seem spacious and uncluttered. The flooring, too, is made from polished concrete, covering both the interiors and the terraces, reinforcing the sense of continuity between inside and outside. Large rocks excavated during construction have been strategically positioned as sculptural elements across the site, as if to challenge the straight geometric lines of the architecture.

The Lake House, 2023
Berlin, Germany

Sigurd Larsen

Berlin is best known for its bustling cityscape, but there are green peninsulas and natural hideouts that provide a different kind of experience. In the context of an adjacent lake, Danish architect Sigurd Larsen's sports facility offers a modern interpretation of a traditional retreat. Inspired by the local vernacular design of the Brandenburg region, the complex evokes the silhouette of boathouses, harmonizing with—or maybe even imitating—the surrounding forest and water. It comprises five staggered timber volumes with pitched roofs, each thoughtfully designed to serve a distinct purpose. The southernmost structure provides guest apartments with panoramic lake views; the central volume is dedicated to communal interaction and houses the open-plan kitchen; the tallest of the five functions as a flexible hall for exhibitions and events; the wellness pavilion offers a sauna and meditation room for relaxation; and the northernmost structure houses therapy studios. The timber construction, with its timber-clad facades, ensures durability and a timeless aesthetic, while the unusual bricolage of wood-framed windows creates large glass facades that bring to mind a modern variation on a treehouse. The dynamic roof pitches create varied interior volumes that offer intimate nooks and open-plan spaces, always keeping in view the forest canopy and lake. Each volume is oriented on the site to catch specific moments of light during the day, further deepening the relationship with nature and the adjacent lake. Tall wooden columns that support the structure from the inside enhance the magical yet restrained treehouse atmosphere.

The Infinite Rise, 2023
Coimbatore, Tamil Nadu, India

Earthscape Studio

The mountain ranges of Tamil Nadu are home to the village of Anaikatti (meaning "a group of elephants"), which is traversed by the Siruvani River, said to have some of the sweetest water in the world. Situated on a natural rock bed, the residence makes use of preexisting land cut about 20 ft (6 m) deep, allowing the semicircular structure to fit naturally into the landscape. A breathtaking view of the deep valley serves as the focal point for orienting the living spaces, further accentuated by an open courtyard that brings natural lighting and gentle ventilation into the structure. As the region often experiences intense winds ranging from unpleasant to harmful, the architects have introduced a gabion wall constructed with locally sourced rocks. As well as shielding the interior from the harsh elements, this design intervention uniquely frames the panorama, creating indirect views that simultaneously expose and hide. The walls between the spaces are crafted from poured earth that was excavated on-site, simplifying construction and reinforcing the circularity of the materials used. Sustainability is at the forefront of the design, with all wooden elements, ranging from doors to furniture, crafted from reclaimed scrap materials. To maintain a cooler temperature, the interior flooring uses Indian Patent Stone—a cement-based flooring material popular in India—finished with green oxide. A well-placed body of water between the rooms and the gabion wall further cools the air that enters the living spaces. Outside, an infinity pool allows swimmers to merge with the valley's mountainous backdrop.

Workshop House, 2022
La Paisanita, Córdoba, Argentina

Agustín Berzero + Manuel Gonzalez Veglia (Tectum Arquitectura)

Solitude, tranquility, and isolation define the Workshop House (Casa Taller) by Agustín Berzero and Manuel González Veglia in the forest and mountain environment of La Paisanita in Argentina's Córdoba region. On the inside, basic functions are accompanied by the comfort of fragrant wood and a fireplace. While the loftlike living and sleeping spaces on the main floor feature large windows that open up toward the surrounding landscape, immersing inhabitants in the cinematic silence of nature, the mezzanine floor above provides an intimate space to work and write, with only a small square window possibly distracting from the task at hand. Full introspection is supported by the diffused light from the lower floor. Structurally, the slim, rectangular volume is made of exposed concrete and rests on lightweight stilts, allowing the landscape underneath to remain unspoiled by construction. Conceptually, the stilts run up the building and divide the volume into four equal sections, finally resulting in a raised square structure—think of Sol LeWitt's *Open Cube* artworks—that crowns the terrace and adorns the monolithic facade. The house is accessed by crossing a bridge that connects the mountain to the terrace, linking to a staircase that runs down the retaining back wall—an entrance that further enhances the feeling of being far off the beaten track and nestled into nature in a contemplative, protective setting, strong yet gentle. Last but not least, a stunning view of the mountains and lush vegetation all around makes it possible to observe the changing light conditions throughout the day while listening to the river below.

Bridgehampton Beach House, 2022
Bridgehampton, New York, USA

Steven Harris Architects

In the serene dunes of Bridgehampton, New York, Steven Harris Architects have imagined oceanfront living for an executive couple from New York. The 12,000-ft^2 (1,115-m^2) home draws inspiration from midcentury modernism and the organic forms of Oscar Niemeyer and Roberto Burle Marx, the Brazilian landscape architect best known for the Copacabana promenade. Its unusual upside-down layout sees public spaces located on the second floor, capitalizing on the panoramic dune and ocean setting. The clients, who are very social, required a summer escape with space for both entertainment and family living. Extensive floor-to-ceiling glass windows flood the interior with natural light and connect the inhabitants to the surrounding landscape during moments shared with friends and family. Orthogonal geometries define the main structure and are complemented by biomorphic shapes, such as the pebble-shaped pavilion and pool, creating a varied interplay between straight lines and organic forms. The pool pavilion's roof doubles as a rainwater-collecting eye-catcher, reflecting the sky and enhancing the home's sustainability. Internally the residence boasts luxurious materials including travertine, Carrara marble, and rainbow onyx, adding elegance and warmth. The furniture is cozy and colorful, with appliqué lighting and design details that create an inviting atmosphere. Art plays a significant role; every room features paintings, site-specific pieces, and sculptures that convey personality. A surprising yet entertaining feature is the indoor basketball court, allowing for private matches between friends and the family's children.

Villa Varoise, 2020
Côte d'Azur, France

NADAAA

In the rural heart of France's Var region, Villa Varoise reimagines the family home as both refuge and landform. The large, austere residence emerges from the earth as sculpted concrete forms that contrasts with the contours of the hillside, its monolithic presence quietly echoing the stone vernacular of the Provençal landscape. The home is oriented towards a vaulted threshold – an extension of the courtyard beyond, and a shaded forum that anchors the structure both spatially and socially. Referencing the centuries-long tradition of courtyards in various cultures, the central void creates a microclimate, framing sky and terrain while connecting the interior and exterior realms. From the courtyard, the dwelling unfolds into a communal upper wing with main functions including the kitchen, living spaces, and the principal bedrooms, all featuring particular viewpoints. A lower extension provides additional sleeping quarters and a family room, all connected by a long street corridor with windows looking into the pool. Material expression is grounded and deliberate. Board-formed concrete walls, local stone, and pale timber surfaces lend the house a tactile permanence, while the green roof, planted with regional species, further integrates the structure into its context. The building is passive by design, with deep overhangs, high thermal mass, and rainwater-harvesting systems that support both the house and its cultivated surroundings. Villa Varoise resists trends in favor of clarity and conviction. It is a house designed for longevity—accommodating generations, respecting its setting, and offering a spatial richness that is both elemental and enduring.

The House Under the Ground, 2023
Eindhoven, the Netherlands

WillemsenU

In a picturesque wildflower meadow bordering a protected nature reserve, WillemsenU has crafted a residence that is as much a part of the landscape as the trees and hills it inhabits. The House Under the Ground is a masterful and creative response to the challenge of integrating architecture into a sensitive environment while providing a sanctuary for its inhabitants. The strategy adopted to replace the goat shed that formerly occupied the site was to practically bury the new dwelling, sinking two of its three floors into the earth and covering the exposed portion with a green hill. This approach minimizes the home's visual impact and also enhances its thermal performance, as the earth's natural insulation maintains a comfortable indoor climate year- round. Internally, each level of the house has its own character and distinct relationship to the surrounding landscape, with some being visible from the outside while others are hidden or even, like the bedroom, completely buried. Natural light reaches these spaces through a central void illuminated by a glass staircase and lift, to ensure the home remains bright despite its underground orientation and is accessible by wheelchair. Aesthetics and sustainability played a role in choosing the right material palette. The facade features rhythmically board-marked concrete, wooden slats reminiscent of the goat shed, and Corten steel, all of which create a contrast to the surrounding meadow without seeming hostile. Inside, concrete surfaces are complemented by warm wooden accents, a tactile counterpart to the cool, sculptural forms of the architecture.

House in Sotogrande, 2024
Sotogrande, Cádiz, Spain

Fran Silvestre Arquitectos

In the exclusive enclave of Sotogrande—the largest privately owned development in Andalusia, located around 310 miles (500 km) south of Madrid—the architects have designed a residence that embodies the essence of minimalist architecture. The design revolves around the synergy of light and shadow that emerges between the roof plane and the zero-elevation plane. The dwelling appears as a large white box, organized visually and spatially by means of the extensive ground floor, the cantilevered roof that provides shade, the expansive glass facades that regulate internal climate, and the warm wooden interiors that offer comfort and privacy. These elements define the living experience and create a connection with the surrounding landscape while giving shelter from the region's intense sun and rain. Accessing the dwelling from above, visitors are greeted by an extensive water mirror on the roof that serves as both visual focal point and thermal insulator; its reflective surface absorbs heat during the day and releases it at night, cutting down the need for artificial heating and cooling mechanisms. Inside, warm-toned materials in white and beige hues, including natural stone and wood, have been prioritized. The layout is built around a central core that allows vertical circulation and access to the roof and is naturally lit by skylights. On the ground-floor terrace, a generous infinity pool looks over the adjacent golf course, enhancing the sense of openness and providing unobstructed views of the landscape.

La Hoja Sobre el Cerro, 2024
Barichara, Santander, Colombia

Alsar-Atelier + GB Urban Studio

Barichara, a town in northern Colombia, is well known for its colonial architecture and cobbled streets. La Hoja Sobre el Cerro (the Leaf on the Hill) embraces tradition as well as the necessary innovation to keep it relevant today. The site on which the volume sits has a complex topography; hence the idea of treating the summer house like a leaf that would gently land on the hilltop, finding its perfect, stable position without disturbing or impacting the natural landscape. One of the house's central features is its double-sloped roof, crafted from recycled clay tiles arranged diagonally to facilitate water runoff. Beyond their practicality, the tiles are a timeless continuation of Colombia's colonial architecture. Local craftsmanship and materials are featured throughout the house, making it seem authentically at ease with its surroundings. The use of local know-how and industry has helped keep emissions as low as possible while promoting Colombian design. On the inside, rather than relying only on walls, the space is organized through level changes that follow the steep slope of the site. The result is a flexible floor plan that is neither fully open nor fully separated, but instead fosters a relationship between its different areas. Wooden elements such as windows, roof cladding, and inbuilt furniture systems radiate warmth and connect the modern house to the surrounding forests and nature. Built-in elements such as the kitchen, benches, and small staircases, which can be used as shelving or for sitting, create a natural yet orderly atmosphere that has a soothing effect.

The Point, 2022
Hobart, Tasmania, Australia

Tanner Architects

How to insert architecture into a context as wild and rural as the crest of a hill within the farmlands of southern Tasmania? By doing as little as possible, but doing it well. In the vision of Tanner Architects, the Point functions as a vessel enabling the experience of the landscape around it. This vision is not only aesthetic but technical, as the dwelling needs to perform impeccably when it comes to durability to withstand the strong elements of the region. Whereas in other summer houses it is paramount to create pockets of shade in outdoor spaces, here the terraces are exposed to the sun but sheltered from the wind. The formal simplicity of the structure underscores the landscape even further; the cantilevered roof rests on the five outer walls, soaring out protectively and adding nothing nonexistential to the landscape, reflecting a noninterventionist approach. Extensive use of glass allows light to permeate the space continuously throughout the day, creating a light show within the building—a feature that works for daytime hours and during the night, as the nearest source of light pollution is miles away. The structure radiates an honest expression and authenticity that are directly linked to the clarity of the materials used: concrete, glass, timber, steel, and stone. It is set subtly into the hillside so that it appears to emerge directly from the land, minimizing its visual footprint while enhancing its bond with the terrain. And so this summer dwelling strikes a breathtaking balance among seclusion, safety from the elements, and elegant immersion in one of the world's most extraordinary wild landscapes.

Bunkie on the Hill, 2024
Muskoka, Ontario, Canada

Dubbeldam Architecture + Design

Bunkie on the Hill, designed by Dubbeldam Architecture + Design, is a minimalist woodland retreat immersed in the forest of central Ontario. The Muskoka region is known for its abundant wildlife, and visitors can spot moose, beavers, and blue herons while engaging in the region's rich offering of sports and adventure activities. Conceived as a contemplative refuge for a multigenerational family, this 1,000-ft^2 (93-m^2) structure offers a compact yet well-designed reinterpretation of the Canadian A-frame cabin. The design's defining gesture is its dynamic roofline, in which two gables intersect as if embracing each other. The orientation is decided by vista; on one side, generous openings provide a lookout onto the adjacent lake, while the other side offers a more sheltered exposure toward the forest. Geometric windows are situated in unexpected places, creating an interplay of light and shadow throughout the day. This strengthens the impression of being immersed in nature while also influencing the perceived richness and depth of the interior material palette. White wallboards delineate the perimeter walls, red cedar slats clad the ceiling, and maple plywood is used for internal partitions, all contributing to a warm and tactile aesthetic. A mezzanine loft, built-in furnishings, and hidden storage ensure that space is efficiently used. All aspects of the design are centered playfully and thoughtfully around enjoyment, even the built-in mezzanine desk with its magnificent lake views. Seen from the outside at night, the dwelling becomes a little light spectacle, with its illuminated windows reflecting onto the trees all around.

La Torre Bianca, 2020
Gagliano del Capo, Puglia, Italy

Lorenzo Grifantini

In the sun-drenched landscape of southern Puglia, Lorenzo Grifantini's summer home emerges as a refined architectural meditation on memory, place, and simplicity. Located in Gagliano del Capo, within a famous hiking area once traversed by fishermen and merchants, this house was conceived as a familial gathering space—an architectural hub where tradition and contemporary living quietly converge. The dwelling is split into two volumes that unfold around a central courtyard with a pool, referencing Mediterranean and monastic spatial typologies. Its main block contains the living spaces and a striking 40-ft (12-m) tower housing two bedrooms. A separate guest wing, designed to be closed off in the winter for energy efficiency, offers three additional bedrooms. Throughout, the geometry is clean and rigorous yet softened by material warmth and site-specific gestures. Following a loosely Italian tradition, the family wished to root the architecture firmly in its local context; the tower is therefore aligned with the bell tower of the nearby Church of San Rocco, with which it enters into a subtle conversation. The result is a home that feels both enclosed and expansive, intimately connected to its surroundings. Built using traditional techniques, it features thick walls for natural insulation, floors of local Pietra Leccese, and 13-ft-high (4-m-high) ceilings that were especially important to the architect, providing a pleasant atmosphere as well as natural ventilation. White microcement surfaces and custom furniture reflect the restrained Mediterranean palette. Every element, from the orientation of the entrances to the hand-finished detailing, contributes to a cohesive, sensorial architecture rooted deeply in the Salento landscape.

Alma Residence, 2022
Harbour Island, Bahamas

Brillhart Architecture + Garth Sawyer

Pink sand sets the tone on the namesake beach of Harbour Island, which this property overlooks. The narrowness of the plot allows for intimacy and a surprising arrival experience as one ascends the slim walkway that leads to the house. Rather than a single dwelling, the house comprises six different structures that are grouped together, forming an ecology of tropical island pavilions. This innovative composition has multiple advantages. First, it conditions its inhabitants to use outdoor pathways to move between different functions and spaces, ensuring that the outdoor context permeates the experience at all times. This effect is enhanced through operable windows, which easily dissolve the boundary between indoors and outdoors. At the same time, they provide shelter from winds and storms without obstructing the views.

Thanks to the varied positioning of each structure, every space offers distinct qualities in terms of light, breeze, views, and temperature. Striking a balance between comfort and wilderness is never easy, yet in this case, the generous indoor spaces offer a cozy experience that blends seamlessly with the site's natural surroundings, which include more than seventy native palm trees. Grounding the project even more in its local context, red cedar wood has been used for the roof structure, drawing on the island's vernacular architecture, which traditionally features exposed rafters and purlins while allowing for impressive ceiling heights. To ensure the privacy of additional guests, a dedicated pavilion sits at the highest point of the lot, where the surroundings become more junglelike and the sound of sea waves fills the air.

I/O Cabin, 2023
Risør, Norway

Erling Berg

The seaside resort of Risør is one of the oldest towns in southern Norway, where temperatures range from –10° Celsius in winter to approximately 24° in summer. In this fresh climate, architect Erling Berg has realized a minimal wooden cabin that harmonizes living conditions with the surrounding forest and fjords. The house is constructed on stilts, connecting it to the Modernist tradition of midcentury glass-and-steel structures and allowing it to float above the sloping terrain and solid rock with minimal impact on the topography. It comprises three separate volumes arranged on a wooden deck. They are linked by a central atrium with generous openings that frame the natural landscape and invite the outdoors in, responding to the dynamic, ever-changing Norwegian climate. White-painted horizontal wood siding and white-oiled spruce are used throughout all the interiors, combining the feel of 1950s and 1960s coastal cabins with contemporary functionality and prioritizing texture, nature, and brightness. In the kitchen and bathrooms, custom-sized windows frame the play of light and shadow or provide views onto the forest and ocean. On the outside, the cantilevered roof is supported by cross-laminated timber beams, providing a stable yet sustainable solution to shelter the house from the elements while enhancing the light flow of the central atrium. Locally sourced spruce is used for the exterior cladding, giving the cabin a weathered patina and camouflaging it among the trees.

Villa Cava, 2023
Tulum, Mexico

Espacio 18 Arquitectura

In the heart of the Mayan jungle, Espacio 18 Arquitectura unveils Villa Cava, a sculptural residence that seamlessly integrates nature, luxury, and spatial poetry. Designed for a couple from Ottawa, Adrian and Andrea, the villa draws inspiration from the famous Cenote Suytun in Yucatán—one of the region's iconic limestone formations that expose groundwater underneath, forming hidden water-filled caverns or wells celebrated for their magical interplays of light, water, and stone. The architectural form emerges as a fortress made of raw, wood-formed concrete. Its brutalist silhouette contrasts with, and is softened by, the thick surrounding greenery. Light and hurricane resistance have been prioritized in the design. Strategic skylights, one of which allows views into the circular glass-bottomed pool above the lobby, infuse the interiors with natural light and cast mesmerizing reflections onto the walls. Special attention has been paid to the site's existing trees, allowing them to dictate the layout and ensuring the structure harmonizes with its environment despite its size and shape. The monochromatic palette of concrete walls flows throughout the interior and exterior of the villa, offering a multisensory experience and highlighting architectural features such as cutouts, columns, and sculptural staircases.
On the ground floor, a study provides space to work while a spacious chef's kitchen with adjacent social areas ensures the success of large dinners and gatherings, potentially spilling out onto the terrace and pool. Interior designer Kayla Pongrác has complemented the architectural vision and concrete composition with a warm, minimalist aesthetic, using maple wood to create a welcoming atmosphere.

Whistling Wind Island, 2023
Pointe au Baril, Ontario, Canada

Akb Architects

Whistling Wind Island is a truly unique retreat situated in the harshly beautiful region of Pointe au Baril, Ontario, where Precambrian rock archipelagos meet the unpredictable forces of nature. Designed by Akb Architects, this remote getaway comprises a cluster of four cedar-clad structures, each scaled to the island's one-acre size and harmoniously integrated into the terrain. It can be reached only by boat and is bound to the seasons, as the lake freezes in November, rendering the island inaccessible. The main cottage is situated at the highest elevation and is complemented by a bunkie, sauna, and boat storage, all connected to each other by wooden plank gangways traversing the rocky outcrops. Together they can sleep eight people. Set against the panoramic openness of the archipelago, the splitting of the volumes fosters a sense of intimacy and connection with the natural surroundings. The architecture responds to the island's mercurial weather patterns with asymmetrical forms and deeply recessed windows, providing shade and reducing solar heat gain. Triple-pane operable glass walls facilitate natural ventilation, while overhangs carved into the building mass offer protection from the elements. Internally, the use of local materials such as Muskoka granite and whitewashed cedar boards creates a sleek yet warm and organic atmosphere. The classic distinction between front and back completely dissolves in the dwellings, as all spaces are designed to capture panoramic views and support a seamless connection between interior and exterior. A deliberate absence of exterior lighting pays tribute to the night sky, avoids light pollution, and allows for romantic evenings dictated by natural rhythms.

San Bruno Beach House, 2024
San Bruno, Yucatán, Mexico

Reyes Ríos + Larraín Arquitectos

The San Bruno Beach House, designed by Reyes Ríos + Larraín Arquitectos, stands as an interaction between solid-void, public-private, open-closed in San Bruno, in the lush paradise of Yucatán, Mexico. The house's rational design harmonizes with its environment through its warm, pink-colored facade, which is in dialogue with the red rocks and desert geology of the region. The architecture features three sequentially arranged volumes on a narrow plot, connected and separated by multiple openings in a hide-and-seek manner. Boundaries between different spatialities are dissolved without giving anything away fully. The rhythmic play of the volumes—composed of concrete, wood, and plaster—creates a dialogue with the land and lets breezes flow freely, while strategically placed apertures frame the ever-changing landscape. The layout is functional: private areas flow into one another while a covered pergola in the central volume provides a meeting point when desired. A critical element in the design is the use of concrete stilts, together with the arrangement of the dwellings behind the second dune, in order to disrupt the natural composition of the site as little as possible. Industrial materials are carefully balanced with bamboo, limestone, and subtropical hardwood to give a modern and innovative appeal while remaining connected to the local context. The pigmented mortar used throughout the exterior and interior spaces has been developed especially for the clients together with a Mexican cement producer, furthering the uniqueness of the summer home. The best views can be enjoyed from the rooftop terrace, which is framed by built-in planters featuring local plant varieties and framing the majestic view over the ocean panorama in front.

Aimasia Residence, 2024
Elia Beach, Mykonos, Greece

A31 Architecture + Tom Dixon

Located in the Elia region on Mykonos, the Aimasia Residence overlooks a popular beach with numerous bars and water-sport facilities. A collaboration by Greek studio A31 Architecture and designer Tom Dixon, the villa reimagines the island's vernacular through a contemporary lens. The design team was especially impressed by the island's geological landscape, leading to a sculptural dialogue between the house and its surroundings. A pre-existing 200-ft-long (62-m-long) dry-stone wall traverses the dwelling, having been preserved as a starting point for the design. This wall evokes the island's traditional agricultural terraces and serves as the property's architectural spine. To the south, the villa overlooks the ever-changing blue of the Aegean Sea, while on the eastern side it frames a dramatic granite hill adorned with UNESCO-listed dry-stone walls. A large infinity pool and two smaller pools adjacent to the bedrooms ensure that guests can enjoy either solitude or company as they please. Internally, the L-shaped layout features full-height sliding glass doors and curved elements that contrast deliberately with the rough exposed concrete. Dixon's design emphasizes tactile materiality and craftsmanship. Each space is thematically divided, reflecting the island's geological identity. Materials such as local stone, minerals, and aluminum are used throughout, with bespoke elements such as plaster bed frames containing soil from the site. The designer has also used the residence to prototype products and test new designs, such as the disk-shaped lights above the large geometrical granite kitchen island, which make for an elegant eye-catcher and possible conversation topic during numerous aperitifs.

Costa Rica Treehouse, 2017
Playa Hermosa, Santa Teresa, Costa Rica

Olson Kundig

Situated within the lush canopy of Costa Rica's Pacific coast, this summer dwelling by Olson Kundig is an architectural ode to immersive, sustainable living. Located near the well-known surf town of Santa Teresa, the three-storey home rises through layers of tropical vegetation, allowing occupants to experience the jungle from the forest floor to the treetops. Constructed almost entirely of locally sourced teak and cenízaro wood, the house is a prime example of site-responsive design—light on the land and rich in texture. Its layout also responds to the natural context. The ground level connects directly to the earth, while the main living spaces are elevated in the mid-canopy, allowing residents to float amid wildlife and verdant foliage. The uppermost floor offers dramatic views of the Nicoya Peninsula, creating a fluid passage from the dense jungle to the expansive horizon. All levels are open-air, embracing the climate and making use of Costa Rica's natural breezes for passive cooling. One of the home's defining features is its operable shutter system, crafted from slender wooden slats. These allow the house to breathe while shading it from the sun yet can close tightly for security or storm protection. An overhanging roof also shelters the interiors from rain and intense sun, reinforcing the home's environmental responsiveness. Sustainable choices have been integral to the design. A rooftop solar array provides power, and a rainwater-collection system supports off-grid water needs—making the Costa Rica Treehouse not only a home but a thoughtful meditation on living within, rather than against, nature.

Falésia D'El Rey House, 2023
Óbidos, Portugal

[i]da arquitectos

Set against the rugged Atlantic coast near the resort area of Praia D'El Rey, this residence by [i]da arquitectos engages directly with the drama of its site: windswept cliffs, expansive sea views, and the ever-changing coastal light. It is both a secure retreat from the elements and a front-row observation hub onto the sea, necessarily balancing openness and protection. The architectural strategy comprises two orthogonally interlocking volumes that create a spatial dramaturgy, structuring the movement of the site. The lower of the two is realized in sand-toned concrete. Protected from wind and uninvited views, it acts as a platform from which the house rises. The upper volume is quite the opposite clad in lighter tones and elevated above the site, it is oriented to capture sweeping ocean views and natural light from the west.

The walkable roof doubles as a viewing platform and terrace. At the heart of the house lies a central 10 m × 10 m courtyard, a protected garden space that offers intimacy and calm amid the exposed coastal context. This internal patio serves as the stage on which domestic life plays out, providing light and ventilation while enhancing the sensory quality of the home. Geometric shapes and openings are key; interspersed glazed side-facades and balconies offer panoramic views and opportunities for hidden retreat. The rigid outlines of the dwelling play with materiality and restraint against nature's abundant setting with an architecture that employs a palette of muted tones and raw finishes, allowing the textures of concrete, stone, and wood to resonate with the surrounding landscape.

Heatherhill Beach House, 2024
Vejby, Gribskov, Denmark

Norm Architects

Around 30 miles (50 km) north of Copenhagen sits Vejby, a small town on the Baltic Sea overlooking the strait of Kattegat, which separates Denmark from Sweden. In this setting, the architects have realized a Nordic oasis. The main themes of the residential dwelling are tranquility and longevity; it is a place where time passes differently and stress is left behind. Wood is the protagonist among the materials and allows the environment and the construction to blend seamlessly. On the outside, cedar cladding adorns the strict parallel lines, which resemble a barn-structure profile while being inherently modern at the same time. Walkways overgrown with grass invite visitors to stop and contemplate nature. As time passes, the external cedar walls will develop a silver patina that complements the sedum roofs and the surrounding environment. Inside, a tone-on-tone material palette continues the journey of calming minimalism. Large windows perfectly frame the outdoor scenery, making the house feel like an observatory. Douglas fir wood and traditional brick flooring are used throughout all interior spaces, while specific elements are made of travertine stone. The mood is harmonious; features such as the simple, impactful stone kitchen island and the embedded fireplace echo the elegance of nature, merging Danish architectural tradition with contemporary style. While the house is large and welcoming, special attention has been paid to creating intimate spaces for introspection, contemplation, and nature gazing. In the bathroom, an extra-large concrete bathtub offers scenic views through a full-frame window positioned right in front of it. For those wishing to enjoy nature, the outdoor shower can be accessed directly from here.

Coral Pavilion, 2022
Ilashe, Lagos, Nigeria

Oshinowo Studio

On the serene Ilashe Peninsula, accessible only by boat from Lagos, Oshinowo Studio has crafted the Coral Pavilion—a minimalist beach retreat that reimagines tropical Modernism through a distinctly Nigerian lens. Designed by Tosin Oshinowo, the pavilion replaces an existing beach house from the 1970s and serves as an escape from the notorious urban hustle of Lagos, a city of 15.9 million people. The pavilion is defined by its simplicity, featuring clean lines, whitewashed walls, and a pleasant balance between poolside relaxation and immersion in nature. Conceived as a day-trip getaway destination, it offers all the necessary comforts without truly permanent sleeping options. Strategic openings and overhangs generate dynamic patterns of shade, especially on the large terrace where olive-green cement furniture provides an eye-catching color detail. A floating coral-pink deck contrasts with the turquoise pool, the golden-yellow sand of the beach, and an outdoor shower with curved yellow pipework. Internally, the pavilion is organized into a linear layout with a kitchen to the east, a central dining area, and a sheltered section to the north housing bathrooms and a kitchen. Living and dining spaces are open-plan and extend onto the elevated pool terrace, designed to offer unobstructed views of the beach. The Coral Pavilion is a testament to the power of simplicity, context-driven design, and a playfulness that sparks joy and pleasure in the daily use of the dwelling. By pairing local materials and references with contemporary simplicity, Oshinowo has designed a space both modern and rooted in its Nigerian setting.

House of Courtyards, 2022
Dubai, UAE

Studio VDGA

The House of Courtyards is Studio VDGA's first project in Dubai. The architects deliberated for a long time over which style to base their proposal on, taking into account the diversity of structures built in the recent past. The completed building aims to reflect ancient desert architecture, with Emirati and Indian influences merging in its design. Spanning about 32,000 ft^2 (3,000 m^2), the residence comprises a comprehensive program of rooms, multiple courtyards, outdoor spaces, meditative nooks, and flowing water, offering a serene oasis within the dynamic urban landscape. Inspired by the region's historic mud-brick structures, its design features a series of interlocking square volumes with rough-hewn sandstone facades, bringing the aesthetics of desert dwellings into a different scale. The sun's path as well as the summer and winter solstices have been closely studied and followed to provide passive cooling amid high temperatures. Other strategies applied to this end include massing in elevations to provide shading and high turrets that function as light shafts without allowing heat to permeate the interiors. Perforated Corten steel screens are used inside and out, allowing for natural ventilation and reducing solar gain. The material palette across the meditative interiors is restrained, incorporating white marble floors and walls and hand-chiseled sandstone from the Indian desert. Rooted in the principles of Vastu Shastra, the home's spatial organization reflects cultural and spiritual considerations, with the central courtyard serving as the *Brahmasthan*—the central point of the home.

The House at Lizard Island, 2022
Great Barrier Reef, Australia

JDA Co.

In 1770, the explorer Captain James Cook visited the indigenous island of the Dingaal people, where the only animals he saw were lizards, giving the island its current name. It is a truly secluded location in Australia's Great Barrier Reef region, which had a population of only sixty-five at the time of the 2021 census. The House at Lizard Island is situated in this extraordinary context, overlooking the Coral Sea from the island's edge. The magic of the site is of great importance to its owners, Steve and Jane Wilson, and the island has inspired the interior of the generous dwelling. It sweeps into the living space and, as they put it, "makes it act as a frame to its surroundings." The floor plan outline resembles the form of one of the stingrays that swim in the sea only a few feet away and inside, the reinforced concrete staircase and the kitchen counter made from emerald quartzite resemble a shell and a conch. The choice of materials has been extremely important for both stylistic and practical reasons. As Lizard Island is exposed to cyclonic winds, it requires a strong concrete structure, while contrasting stone flooring brings a more natural feel to the terraces and ground floor. Narrow slit windows on the south and west sides allow for cooling breezes during the summer and can be closed off with copper blades that line the exterior in case of storms. Rosewood and copper are also used for the interiors, keeping things simple while creating a warm impression. Particular importance has been given to framing the surrounding vistas, and each of the three bedrooms looks out onto a specific site.

In the high plains of San Luis Potosí, famous for its colonial architecture and a particularly young demographic, Casa JN stands as a testament to the harmonious and flexible integration of architecture with the natural surroundings, composed of desert scrub and oak forest. Designed by Estudio Hidiin in collaboration with Tres Puntos Arquitectura, the residence spans nearly 14,000 ft^2 (1,300 m^2) and is constructed using local materials that reflect the region's rich cultural heritage. A key element of the design is the central courtyard featuring an apple tree, which serves as a symbol for the cyclical nature of life and brings the notion of the passage of time into the house. The architects describe the courtyard as "a concatenation of surprises" around which the living areas are organized, promoting a feeling of togetherness and continuity. The residence is arranged across three levels and features an expansive footprint to accommodate the needs of an evolving family, while its modular architectural program ensures it will continue to adapt over time. It oscillates between more robust outdoor zones and elegant interior spaces with large windows, such as the double-height main hall. Highlighting craftsmanship, the interiors feature bespoke woodwork and details that pay homage to Mexican tradition while relying on elemental contrasts defined by volcanic stone, marble, and steel. Collaborations with local artisans have resulted in unique pieces such as desks and wall sculptures, adding character and a decorative, homey atmosphere grounded in sensorial experience.

Hale Mau'u, 2020
Hawaii, USA

Walker Warner

Hale Mau'u, a serene five-bedroom retreat in Hawaii, is divided into multiple separate volumes, giving it an airy and non-imposing architectural appearance. The name of the property translates to "House in the Grass," and its garden spaces, planted with local shrubs and long grass, were designed in collaboration with landscape architect David Y. Tamura Associates. The clients' request was to avoid typical resort architecture and create a house unlike any other. The site itself is unusual for Hawaii: situated where arid plains prevail rather than the tropical rainforest the island is known for, it commands views of both the ocean and the volcanic mountains. Shallow-pitched roofs with standing copper seams make the structure stand out immediately while also sheltering the wooden perimeter walkways around each volume. Visitors navigate the desert garden of volcanic rock and native vegetation on a raised boardwalk that connects the four structures. This layout, together with the moody surrounding landscape, creates an atmosphere reminiscent of a small village, offering the choice of privacy or togetherness within the expansive site. Barn-style cypress doors slide open to create natural ventilation and connect the Catherine Kwong-designed interiors to the wider site. Inside, polished concrete floors and exposed steel columns combine with warmer elements such as cypress-wood ceilings, custom ceramics, and lighting design by Anna Kondolf. At the end of the boardwalk, an exposed concrete pool and spa complete the experience.

Estancia San José, 2024
Alaior, Menorca, Spain

Atelier du Pont

Estancia San José is a transformative project by Atelier du Pont, in collaboration with Aru Arquitectura, that remakes two dilapidated farm buildings into a vacation home for a mother-and-daughter duo looking to spend more time together. Located in the sun-drenched hills of Alaior in the Menorcan countryside, the nineteenth-century-farmhouse and adjacent stone barn have been redeveloped into a four-bedroom summer dwelling. The design is rustic yet contemporary, as the architects preserved the original structures and allowed traditional aspects, existing textures, and wall finishes to intertwine with more modern additions. Local Marés limestone and rough-hewn stone walls pay homage to Menorca's architectural vernacular, while elements from Africa, the Middle East, and Patagonia reference places where the owners have previously called home. Interior spaces are defined by a harmonious blend of materials: terra-cotta floors, natural stone washbasins, and bespoke furniture pieces such as rope-woven headboards and terra-cotta side tables designed by the architects. The kitchen, situated in the main farmhouse, features handmade acid-yellow ceramic tiles from Mallorca, taking inspiration from a pale yellow ceiling that has been uncovered in one of the other volumes. Large interventions have been made where necessary to change the function and feel of the space; in the barn, which originally featured only one window, a series of doors onto a sunny terrace now provides light and air circulation. So that the home and its Mediterranean garden of wild olive trees and aromatic garigue can be enjoyed throughout the seasons, the property includes a hammam as well as an outdoor pool.

Oeiras House, 2024
Oeiras, Lisbon, Portugal

OODA

Among the undulating hills of Oeiras, a town and municipality in the western Lisbon metropolitan area on the Portuguese Riviera, OODA has crafted a residence that transcends challenging topography to offer a superb living experience. Spanning 3,768 ft^2 (350 m^2), Oeiras House integrates an imaginative and complex architectural strategy with its natural context. The design circles the site's westward slope, which initially posed limitations in natural light. Rather than viewing this as a constraint, OODA developed a U-shaped layout that maximizes daylight exposure and creates sheltered outdoor spaces. This configuration cleverly resolves the site, ensuring privacy and boosting scenic connections between the interior and the surrounding landscape. A central patio serves as the heart of the home. Partially embedded in the terrain, it is illuminated by a mosaic-tiled pool and overlooked by the sloping topography of a garden with rocks and wild rosemary. Materiality is key to the home's design. The upper volume, constructed from exposed concrete, provides structural integrity and aesthetic appeal thanks to a strong rationalistic geometry. By contrast, the lower-level interiors incorporate natural textures such as wood along with a midcentury furniture style. Contrasts feature throughout: an unexpected stainless steel kitchen is paired with wood paneling, balancing austerity with warmth. Large glazed openings frame both sides of the living area, strengthening the synergy between indoor and outdoor spaces. Creating an inviting living environment through the novel application of topography, materiality, and spatial organization, OODA's design is a Modernist statement that remains forward-thinking in its approach.

Casa Cabrita Moleiro, 2021
Vale d'el Rei, Lagoa, Portugal

Atelier Data

Atelier Data's transformation of Casa Cabrita Moleiro reimagines a former family-run granary mill into a five-bedroom holiday home that celebrates the rural heritage of Portugal's Algarve region. Situated on elevated terrain in Vale d'el Rei, the project preserves and repurposes existing structures including a windmill, threshing floor, and livestock corral, integrating them into a cohesive residential complex. The design incorporates local vernacular architecture, reinterpreting the *açoteia algarvia*—a roof terrace traditionally used for drying fresh produce and observing the sea. The former walls of the mill have been integrated with the new program, unified by whitewashed color. Throughout, geometric shapes and carved-out voids create private spaces for the bedrooms, which are arranged around a windowless central courtyard. All balconies, terraces, and other openings face outward, framing vistas of the surrounding arid landscape and the Atlantic Ocean. The property's two main volumes can be used independently. Three en suite bedrooms are located in the first volume, offset from the former exterior wall of the miller's house, forming a sequence of courtyards that provide private outdoor spaces. Above, a rooftop terrace with a shared Jacuzzi takes full advantage of the sea view. The second volume houses two additional en suite bedrooms. Locally sourced, recycled, or exposed materials are used throughout, including the reclaimed railway track wood laid in playful patterns on the patio pavement and terrace spaces. Exposed structural concrete ceilings, also whitewashed, contribute to the home's minimalist, rural character, while polished concrete floors introduce a contemporary aesthetic indoors.

Boa Vista House, 2023
Porto Feliz, São Paulo, Brazil

Studio Arthur Casas

On a generous plot of land in São Paulo, a luxurious program of six bedrooms, a gym, kitchen, dining, wellness, and living areas is cleverly arranged within a long, narrow volume, which had to remain unchanged due to setback restrictions. Using sloping roofs and nonperpendicular angles, the architects have succeeded in bringing movement into the shape and creating a range of differently framed internal lines of sight. What gives the house an especially pleasant ambience are the generous, simple interior spaces, designed in such a way as to guarantee their continuation outdoors. The same materials are used inside and out: carbonized pine wood as cladding, porcelain flooring, and Moledo—a soft, granitelike rock, popular in Brazil due to its unique beauty—for the walls. The wall of the gourmet area, where cooking and tasting take place on the same kitchen island, incorporates special Ipsilon *cobogós* designed by the architects, allowing light and ventilation to enter the space softly. Attention has been paid to diffused light and earth-toned colors; the wellness and sauna area on the floor below is connected to the pool through glass, bringing scenographic reflections into the area and helping to create a relaxed atmosphere. Most of the bedrooms are located on the upper floor, where shading is provided through tilting windows clad in carbonized pine wood on both the interior and exterior. These grant privacy and tranquility for long sleepers while also creating a geometric effect on the outdoor facade when opened all at once.

Topless House, 2020
Le Pouliguen, Loire Atlantique, France

Avignon Architecte

Overlooking France's Atlantic coast in Le Pouliguen, a short drive from Nantes, Avignon Architecte's Topless House redefines the concept of the summer retreat through bold simplicity and spatial ingenuity. A formerly dilapidated veranda has been transformed and finally replaced by a 50-m^2 extension to the main summer home. At the core of this transformative design is a retractable Corian roof—the architectural flourish that gives the house its name. When extended, the roof creates an overhanging cantilever, resulting in a charming shaded open shelter suited to long, conversational dinners. When it is retracted, the entire space opens directly to the sky. This smart and theatrical mechanism allows the house to breathe with the rhythms of its environment, maximizing the possibilities of the small space by offering sun, air, and openness whenever desired.

Internally, the program is minimalist and meticulously composed. A 23-ft-long (7-m-long) kitchen runs the length of the space, flowing into a bedroom designed as an intimate "cottage within a cottage." A narrow corridor, Hellenistic in style, doubles as an entrance and much-needed storage spine. The entire south facade opens via Vitrocsa sliding glass panels, erasing the boundary between the kitchen and a polished concrete terrace. Every detail—sandblasted glass, concealed lighting under the moving roof, and carefully articulated material transitions—contributes to a sense of seamless continuity. Elegance and poetry go hand in hand with function and technology in the small dwelling. In the Topless House, architecture is not a shell but a mechanism of immersion that guides its inhabitants' views and movements from across the site toward the seaside.

Casa Chimera, 2023
Orbetello, Ansedonia, Italy

Daniele Marcotulli Architect

Situated off the coast of southern Italy, Casa Chimera is a transformative renovation of a 1990s organic-style residence by architect Oreste Martelli Castaldi. Commissioned by a young entrepreneur seeking a multifaceted property, the project by Daniele Marcotulli reimagines the home as a space for both relaxation and entertainment. The design places the kitchen at the center and adds completely new features, including a home cinema, a lounge area, and guest accommodations. Straight and circular neon ceiling lights alternate as a bold lighting solution in all spaces, contrasting with the wooden flooring and ceiling paneling while creating interesting reflections on the newly inserted mirrors and ceramics. Despite the extensive updates to the living spaces and the addition of contemporary, more conve nient amenities, the essence of Casa Chimera remains intact.

Simple, modernist shapes radiate a serene energy which floods the open-plan layout and seamlessly connects interior spaces with views of the surrounding landscape. The choice of materials plays on a balance of roughness and refinement: In the fitness area, raw wooden ceilings echo the timber floorboards of the upper floors, while the mirrored surfaces amplify light and space. The downstairs living space features a sand-colored resin floor that establishe a chromatic continuity with the outdoor spaces covered in terracotta tiles. Materials used in the bedrooms echo the palette of the common areas, with wood, resin, and mirrors enhancing the impression of the space. Guests can come together around the sculptural kitchen island or the fireplace area, both made from yet another material: basalt stone.

Primeriza House, 2021
Matanzas, VI Región, Chile

Stanaćev Granados Arquitectos

Located in a coastal village in central Chile, this large family home is focused on joyful activities and the tranquility of nature. The volume has a solid concrete base that holds a garage and storage space while strengthening the house against the strong winds that arise from the Pacific Ocean just in front of the cypress-filled plot. Two light-filled floors rise from the base, both equipped with floor-to-ceiling windows all the way around that provide breathtaking views of the ocean and surrounding hills, as well as a constant opportunity to observe the changing conditions outside from every corner of the living space. The effect of being within a very generous tree house is further enhanced by the wooden structure that defines the volume both structurally and visually, giving it a notable lightness and organic look. While the lower floor and sea-facing terrace are made from dark-stained wood, the upper floor contrasts with gentle white tones that diffuse light coming from the vertical line of toplights running along the length of the volume. The main floor connects to the upper floor through open-weave cargo netting, installed to be enjoyed by the young children of the owners, to accommodate moments of relaxation with the whole family, and to allow for sharing the space without having to be in the same place. The combination of open double-height spaces, light-flooded interiors, and wooden features makes the dwelling a perfect summer home—even before considering its proximity to the sea and nature, which offer countless outdoor activities.

Beach House Kea, 2024
Kea, Greece

Christos Vlachos + wip architects

Resembling a piece of land art by the likes of Michael Heizer, the beach house emerges as an extension of its environment, situated alongside the shore of Kea, a small island in the Cyclades archipelago in the Aegean Sea. The architects have transformed the structure, once a stone warehouse for maritime trade, into a luxurious summer residence that keeps in mind local heritage and values the surrounding landscape. The building is integrated into the hillside and features linear, winding volumes that follow and contrast the natural contours of the terrain and coastline. Stones from the original building have been reused for continuity, while new walls have been constructed using the traditional dry-wall technique widely seen in the Mediterranean. Green roofs filled with local plant varieties further help to make the house mimetic. Within them, skylights have been introduced, providing additional light for a lush indoor garden that connects the living space to the kitchen. Interior spaces are characterized by sleek design; dark, earthy colors such as anthracite, gray, and black; and smooth surfaces, providing a tranquil contrast to the tactile richness of the external environment. The program of the dwelling flows mainly around a long main terrace that is perfect for large groups, gatherings, and shared sunbathing. The guest bedrooms are situated separately, allowing for privacy, and the architects have included smaller recreational platforms and staircases throughout to facilitate movement and offer smaller breakout spaces. To ensure minimal environmental impact and off-grid autonomy, the dwelling has its own energy-management system and a domestic desalination unit.

Casa Santa Teresa, 2020
Ajaccio, Corsica, France

Amelia Tavella Architectes

Perched along the storied Route des Sanguinaires in Ajaccio, Casa Santa Teresa is a masterful restoration that bridges time, terrain, and tradition. Originally built in the 1950s, the villa has been reimagined by Corsican architect Amelia Tavella as a serene dialogue between built form and natural surroundings. Tavella's memories of growing up on the island, including family gatherings and summer nights, have guided some of the design decisions. With five bedrooms and multiple terraces across four floors, the architectural structure slowly cascades down toward the beach and the ground-floor shared spaces. Expansive glass openings and pivoting doors dissolve the boundaries between interior and exterior, bathing the living spaces in Mediterranean light and framing ever-shifting views of the sky and sea. Materiality anchors the architecture in its environment. Local stone, pale wood, and handwoven rattan echo the island's raw textures, while soft, organic finishes lend warmth and tactility. The indoor centerpiece of the home is an open-plan living space from which hidden alcoves can be discovered, and the top-floor bedrooms can be reached via a sculptural staircase. Outside, a panoramic terrace with a pool overlooks the beach, making swimming a possible activity even when the sea is rough. Some more typical elements of island architecture, such as rope railings and slatted shutters, incorporate a traditional touch into the villa's contemporary aesthetic. With its terraces, fireplace, and outdoor kitchen, Casa Santa Teresa is a well-executed example of the balance between modernity and memory, between function and poetry, that enriches every seaside summer stay.

Mori House, 2023
Mornington Peninsula, Victoria, Australia

Manuel Aires Mateus

The outcome of an unusual collaboration, Mori House follows a concept design by Portuguese architect Manuel Aires Mateus, realized by MA+Co, for Jeff Provan, director of Neometro, and his wife, Mariko Mori Provan, in Mount Martha, Victoria. The design process began with a brief made of references describing books, music, materials, and how the clients wanted their home to feel, rather than a formal plan of necessary spaces. From this beginning, a magical concrete residence cast in situ emerged, effortlessly bringing together influences from Portugal, Japan, and Australia. The house consists of four sculptural concrete pavilions arranged in a cruciform plan, each framing a unique courtyard: a pool, a grove, a vegetable garden, and a chicken run. These courtyards give structure and rhythm to the home while offering varying degrees of openness and intimacy. A central volume connects the wings and rises to form a lantern-like tower, accessed via a pair of geometric staircases. From this rooftop belvedere, panoramic views stretch across the bay and surrounding landscape. Internally, in this point, the volumes can be opened or divided by large wooden doors. The interiors balance austerity with warmth. A tatami room, raw concrete walls, soft timber finishes, and filtered natural light create an atmosphere that is contemplative yet vividly alive, especially supported by a great collection of books, sculptures and other artworks, furniture, and well-placed lighting that feel casually yet perfectly placed. It is a home shaped not only by its context but by the rituals and patterns of family life.

Shift House, 2023
Menorca, Spain

Nomo Studio

The northern coast of Menorca differs from the more gentle and sandy south of the island with its wild beauty and unique rock formations of red clay. In this setting, Nomo Studio has crafted a refined summer home that transforms a compact site into a luminous three-level retreat. The residence consists of simple rectangular volumes shifted in plan to create a dynamic aesthetic despite the limited size of the plot. Fluted concrete walls sliced by continuous window openings define the villa in horizontal stripes of solid and glass. The heaviness of the grooved concrete block used in the facade generates a gravitational tension with the surrounding 360-degree glazed bands. The day area opens onto an elevated terrace extending into an overflowing pool, all located on the top floor to guarantee the best sea views. Expansive windows look out in all directions and ensure plenty of natural light. In the basement, a sunken patio provides abundant light and ventilation to all three floors and features square columns that connect to the roof. An outer stair leads to a rooftop solarium that unveils panoramic views of the Mediterranean. Internally, roughly polished white concrete flooring and travertine steps combine with simple white walls and khaki-beige microcement in the bathrooms and kitchen. Built-in wardrobes and bathroom furniture feature artisanal rattan and light pine wood carpentry, while glossy wooden details such as handrails and doorsteps bring sparkle to the beach-like interiors. In contrast, the exteriors feature darker wattle ceilings and teak carpentry, granting the villa a sense of sober elegance despite its varied materials.

Al Suave House, 2023
El Zonte, La Libertad, El Salvador

Cincopatasalgato + Pepe Cabrera Homes

Along the Pacific shoreline of El Zonte, on a plot of land that the client purchased more than twenty years ago on his first visit here, is a beachfront retreat that exemplifies a sensitive, elegant approach to the surfer lifestyle. Designed collaboratively by Salvadoran studio Cincopatasalgato and Spanish firm Pepe Cabrera Homes, the five-bedroom villa emphasizes connection—to nature, to materials, and to community. Rather than dominating the landscape, it is broken into two pavilions, positioned to protect mature trees and accommodate a pool that winds through the property like a river. This fluid layout enhances passive ventilation and blurs the line between inside and out, a hallmark of the region's coastal lifestyle. Material choices root the project in its context. Local Honduran wood clads the exterior in rich, textured tones that weather beautifully over time. Salvadoran bricks, Costa Rican glass, travertine floors, and handcrafted clay bathrooms imbue the interiors with warmth and tactility while creating a refined South American aesthetic. The furniture was sourced from European brands imported from Spain and mixed with Salvadoran and Guatemalan designer pieces. More than just a residence, Al Suave House serves as a hub for slow living and collective experiences. Future plans for a yoga studio, organic store, café, and treatment space further this vision, inviting both guests and the wider community to gather, restore, and engage. It is an idea developed over time, starting with the acquisition many years ago during a surfing holiday—when the client was seeking a camping site with reliable trees to grant shadow and the perfect place to read—and ultimately leading to the architects' commission to fulfill the desires of the family and the needs of the local community.

Piil, 2023
Ruu, Jõelähtme Parish, Estonia

Arsenit

The Piil tree house by Arsenit may be one of the smallest summer dwellings in existence, yet it offers a compact and comforting place from which to enjoy nature. Nestled in the serene Estonian forest, it rises 30 ft (9 m) above the ground, which brings it into line with the surrounding treetops. The prefabricated retreat balances on a single leg, resulting in a cantilevered structure that minimizes its footprint and provides panoramic views of the surrounding wilderness. Its structure is modular, hence it can be produced cost-effectively and time-effectively. In addition, the use of steel made material sourcing particularly easy, as the client is a metal manufacturer. Piil is the prototype for what will be four dwellings in total, all arranged to frame sunset views of the nearby Jägala River. The name Piil derives from the Estonian word for "peeking" and reflects the design's intent to offer occupants a unique view into the forest. A hammock mezzanine is installed to relax while gazing through an expansive window-skylight, allowing residents to feel suspended within the treetops, immersed in the movements of the glittering forest foliage. Below, the 205-ft^2 (19-m^2) interior is conceived as a cohesive piece of joinery, crafted entirely from whitewashed oak. This intervention manages to incorporate all necessary features for relaxation and remote work needs into the humble space: a king-size bed, two workstations, a kitchenette, and ample concealed storage. Externally, Piil benefits from untreated, thermally modified pine produced in Estonia, which deepens its connection with the forest, will age well, and filters air and light.

Index

Picture Credits

©Jack Arundell: 26; César Béjar: 166–71,122–5; Peter Bennetts: 162–5; Jeremy Bittermann / JBSA: 58–61; Jonas Bjerre-Poulsen / Norm Architects: 148–51; ©Sylvain Bonniol: 200–3; Tamas Bujnovszky: 36–7; Federico Cairoli: 74–7; Carlo Carossio: 108–13; Luis Díaz Díaz: 28–33; Thibaut Dini for Amelia Tavella: 218–21; Doublespace: 126–9; Serena Eller Vainicher (EllerStudio): 204–7; ©George Fakaros: 214–17; Fisher Studios: 48–51; Alvaro Fonseca - Depth Lens: 10–15; ©Richard Gaston: 24–5, 27; Adam Gibson: 100–3; Stephan Goettlicher: 114–17; Fernando Guerra: 38–41, 92–5, 182–7, 194–9; Fernando Guerra I FG+SG : 144–5,147; Joan Guillamat: 226–9; John Horner: 82–7; Studio IKSHA: 70–3; Ivanhsousa: 146; Bálint Jaksa: 34–5; Mike Kelley: 134–9; Shoayb Khattab: 158, 160 (bottom); Kkrom services: 66–9; Yiorgos Kordakis: 42–7; Erik Lefuander: 52–7; ©Nic Lehoux: 140–3; Yifan Liu: 234–7; Maria Missagli: 76–8; Miguel Nacianceno: 16–19; Cristobal Palma: 20–3; Mateo Perez Photography: 96–9; Eric Petchek: 78–81; Ema Peter: 159, 160 (top), 161; Carlos Rollá: 118–21; Tolu Sanusi: 152–7; Richard John Seymour: 188–93; Riley Snelling: 104–7; ©Edmund Sumner: 130–3; Derek Swalwell: 222–5; Topofilia Studio: 230–3; Architectuurfotograaf - Rob van Esch: 88–91; Marcos Zegers: 208–11.

Phaidon Press Limited
2 Cooperage Yard
London E15 2QR

Phaidon Press Inc.
111 Broadway
New York, NY 10006

Phaidon SARL
55, rue Traversière
75012 Paris

phaidon.com

First published 2026

ISBN 978 1 83729 093 2

A CIP catalogue record for this book is available from the British Library and the Library of Congress.

Commissioning Editor: Emilia Terragni
Project Editor: Caitlin Arnell Argles
Project texts: Izabela Anna Moren
Production Controller: Gif Jittiwutikarn
Design: Philipp Hubert

Printed in China